For Merida and Brooke

still more small poems

by Valerie Worth
pictures by Natalie Babbitt

Farrar, Straus and Giroux   New York

Poems copyright © 1976, 1977, 1978 by Valerie Worth
Pictures copyright © 1978 by Natalie Babbitt
All rights reserved
Published simultaneously in Canada by
McGraw-Hill Ryerson Ltd., Toronto
Printed in the United States of America
First edition, 1978
Library of Congress Cataloging
in Publication Data
Worth, Valerie / Still More Small Poems
[1. American Poetry]
I. Babbitt, Natalie / II. Title
PZ8.3.W913St / 811'.5'4 / 78-11739

still more small poems

door

My grandmother's
Glass front door
Held a fancy pattern
Of panes, their
Heavy edges cut
On a slant: when
Sun shone through,
They scattered
Some eighty little
Flakes of rainbows
Into the room,
Walking the walls,
Glowing like fallen
Flowers on the floor;
Why don't they
Make front doors that
Way any more?

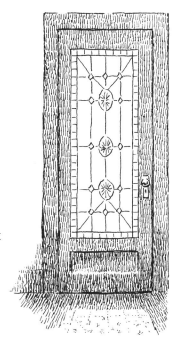

kite

The kite, kept
Indoors, wears
Dead paper
On tight-
Boned wood,
Pulls at the tied
Cord only
By its weight—

But held
To the wind,
It is another thing,
Turned strong,
Struck alive,
Wild to be torn
Away from the hand
Into high air:

Where it rides
Alone,
Glad,
A small, clear
Wing, having
Nothing at all
To do
With string.

turtle

The turtle
Does little
But sleep
On a stone,
Alone
In his glass
Bowl.

Is he bored
By it all?
Does he hope
Something
Will happen,
After a hundred
Naps?

Or is it enough
To wake
Quietly,
Shawled
In the shade
Of his
Shell?

compass

According to
The compass,
Wherever you happen
To stand,

North, south,
East and west,
Meet in the palm
Of your hand.

bell

By flat tink
Of tin, or thin
Copper tong,
Brass clang,
Bronze bong,

The bell gives
Metal a tongue—
To sing
In one sound
Its whole song.

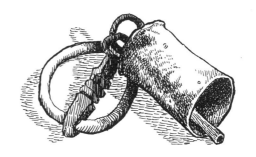

pigeons

The pigeon shed
Is hot, and smells
Of dust and corn;

Pigeon-voices
Bubble, wings scuffle
Above our heads;

We are allowed
To touch the throats
Of the young squabs:

They sink and shift
Like beanbags, heavy
With grain, and warm.

honeycomb

Sealed wax cells
Dull the honey's gold
And hold it stiff and still.

The bees build well,
But the hidden honey
Only waits to spill—

To glitter out free,
And spread itself everywhere,
The way honey will.

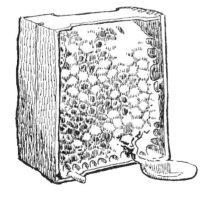

rags

Stuffed away into
An old pillowcase,

Dragged forth again
In crumpled clods,

Torn to wash windows
Or tie up tomato plants,

Thrown out at last—
Poor sad gray wads

That once were faithful
Flannel pajamas,

Favorite pink-
Flowered underpants.

barefoot

After that tight
Choke of sock
And blunt
Weight of shoe,

The foot can feel
Clover's green
Skin
Growing,

And the fine
Invisible
Teeth
Of gentle grass,

And the cool
Breath
Of the earth
Beneath.

mushroom

The mushroom pushes
Its soft skull
Up through the soil,

Spreads its frail
Ribs into full
Pale bloom,

And floats,
A dim ghost,
Above the tomb

Where an oak's
Old dust lies
Flourishing still.

pail

A new pail,
Straight, tight,
Brushed to a cold
Silver shine,

Soon learns
Other ways:
Once filled with
Oats or ashes,

Grayed by rain,
Its handle
Bent, its
Bottom dented,

Grown peaceful
And plain,
It becomes
A real pail.

horse

In the stall's gloom,
His back, curved
Like a high sofa,
Turns on unseen
Legs, looms closer,
Until his long
Head forms above
The door, his face
Of thin silk over
Bone: to be stroked
Carefully, like
Fine upholstery
On a hard chair.

back yard

Sun in the back yard
Grows lazy,

Dozing on the porch steps
All morning,

Getting up and nosing
About corners,

Gazing into an empty
Flowerpot,

Later easing over the grass
For a nap,

Unless
Someone hangs out the wash—

Which changes
Everything to a rush and a clap

Of wet
Cloth, and fresh wind

And sun
Wide awake in the white sheets.

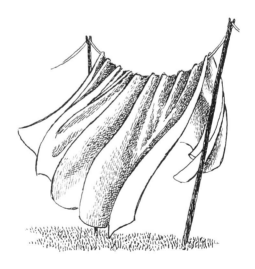

rosebush

In summer it
Blooms out fat
And sweet as milk;

In winter it
Thins to a bitter
Tangle of bones;

And who can say
Which is the
True rosebush?

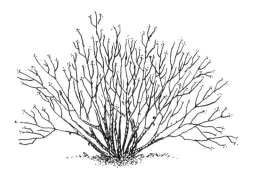

slug

The slug
Slides slyly
By night,

To nibble
The new
Green shoot,

To riddle
The weak
White root—

Hated
By all
But the moon,

Who smiles
On his scenes
Of crime,

And silvers
His trails
Of slime.

rocks

They say, No
Life on the moon,
Not much, if
Any, on Mars—

But I say,
See those
Rocks: how
They stand up

Shapely against
The dust, in
Their subtle
Limbs and skins,

Showing a
Live mineral
Cleverness, just
Like rocks here.

cat bath

In the midst
Of grooming
Her inner
Thigh,

Her leg
Locked
High at
Her back,

She looks
Up: with
A pink
Crescent

Tongue
Left
Between lip
And lip.

tom

Old Tom
Comes along
The room
In steps
Laid down
Like cards,
Slow-paced
But firm,
All former
Temptations
Too humdrum
To turn
Him from
His goal:
His bowl.

roadside

Beside the road,
Narrow strips of
Field still run,
Full of pale
Grass, thin scrub,
Scrap and rust
Of things
Cast away—
A dead glove,
Empty bottle-skulls,
A shivering spirit
Of lost cellophane.

mice

Mice
Find places
In places,

A dark
Hall behind
The hall,

Odd rooms
That other
Rooms hide:

A world
Inside
The wide world,

And space enough,
Even in
Small spaces.

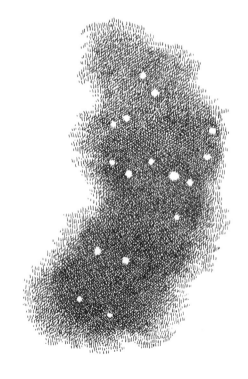

stars

While we
Know they are
Enormous suns,
Gold lashing
Fire-oceans,
Seas of heavy
Silver flame,

They look as
Though they could
Be swept
Down, and heaped,
Cold crystal
Sparks, in one
Cupped palm.

egg

Somehow the hen,
Herself all quirk
And freak and whim,

Manages to make
This egg, as pure
And calm as stone:

All for the sake
Of a silly chick,
Another squawking hen.

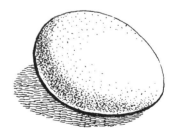

sweets

Here
Is a list
Of likely
Words
To taste:

Peppermint,
Cinnamon,
Strawberry,
Licorice,
Lime:

Strange
How they manage
To flavor
The paper
Page.

garbage

The stained,
Sour-scented
Bucket tips out
Hammered-gold
Orange rind,

Eggshell ivory,
Garnet coffee-
Grounds, pearl
Wand of bared
Chicken bone:

Worked back soon
To still more
Curious jewelry
Of chemical
And molecule.

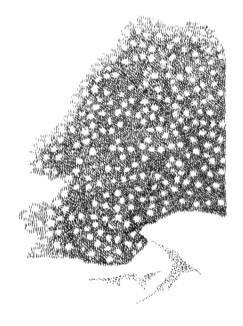

snow

Gardens, fields,
The far hills,
Lie deathly
With white winter,

Wide drifts
And heavy deeps
Made only of
Each snowflake fallen,

Like these many
Still falling, these
Few still alive
On my sleeve—

None anywhere
Ever like
This one, this
Very one.